Brooke,
May God continue to be
a blessing to others. You
bless you through!
can do all things
Christ who strengthens you.
God Bless!

Kerry Stevenson

Inspirations

Inspired by Faith,
Family, Friends & Football.

A book of poetry by
Kerry Stevenson

Inspirations In Life

Copyright © 2018 Kerry Stevenson

® Filthy Physical

Editor copyright © eVision, LLC

ISBN-13: 9780794847104

ISBN-10: 0794847102

Published by
Whitman
Publishing, LLC
PUBLISHING SINCE 1934
www.whitman.com

Whitman Publishing, LLC
1974 Chandalar Drive, Suite D
Pelham, AL 35124

FILTHY PHYSICAL ®

In Loving Memory of my mom, Theresa,
and my grandparents, Hattie Mae and Mason.

Dedication

For Joyce:

For always believing in me. For your undying
love and support. I will always remember the
great example that you lived and how special you
made me feel every day. I love you dearly.

Dedicated to my dude:

Jarvis, you were taken away from
me way too soon, but your loving and
outgoing spirit will forever live in me.
You showed me how to live and
enjoy life, and I am forever grateful.

Contents

Inspirations in Life

Inspirations in Life is a book of poetry inspired by God and His presence in my life. I've been affected by a number of life's lessons. God has helped me to use situations involving circumstances in my life to help me to motivate, influence and inspire others through the wisdom He has given me.

Four areas that have contributed to making me who I am today are FAITH, FAMILY, FRIENDS and FOOTBALL. My life has included these four elements for as long as I can remember. These four elements have been the driving force behind the expressions in *Inspirations in Life*. I want to share these same experiences with you that I have shared with many family members, friends and sometimes even strangers, as the Spirit leads me to do so. I share my experiences to encourage others, ensuring them to believe that it's not as bad as you think; we need to have a little faith, and there's no better feeling than that of being loved, and that of sharing special moments with the ones we love.

God gave me the gift of writing poetry to help me to express the way I feel in situations of love, fun and family. The poetry I write illuminates the responses to my four inspirations of faith, family, friends and football. I pray that you can connect to at least one piece as you read this spirit-filled book of poetry and that you use these words of inspirations to influence, encourage and be a blessing to others as I aim to serve you through God's influence in my life.

Thank you for allowing me to share this inspirational poetry motivated by my love for faith, family, friends and football.

– Kerry Stevenson

Inspired by Faith

Inspired by Faith

Faith, to me, is a belief in a manner where you trust in God. What does it mean to be inspired by your faith? *Merriam-Webster's Dictionary* suggests faith is a "belief and trust in and loyalty to God." So, to be inspired by faith is to be moved by a God that I trust and believe in.

Growing up, I lived next door to the church I attended and was raised in. We learned things like the books of the Bible and the author of each book. We also learned some important phrases and verses in the Bible. These verses shared stories where God fed the hungry, gave water to the thirsty and He even woke a man up from the dead. He himself was killed an innocent man, hung on a cross, died, and arose from the dead with all power in heaven and on earth in His hands. I don't think this is such a bad person to put your faith in. Elvester Turner, my pastor in my youth, was a good man of God and he taught us the things we needed to have in order get to heaven.

I still remember those things today. It is on this belief that I love, teach, motivate, inspire, and coach individuals and team members to believe, trust, and be grateful for our God and His great works. The poetry I write allows my faith to shine through as I counsel, encourage and provide prayers to the audience I serve. My faith inspired me to write the poems in the following section.

Living My Blessed Life

Up early in the mornings,
No heartaches and no strife.
Thanking my Lord for favor,
And presence in my life.

Thanks for allowing me,
To see another day.
And also for protecting me,
When dangers came my way.

I'm Living My Blessed Life,
Thanks God for all You do.
You brought me through the storms of life,
I owe it all to You.

Now I can praise You when the sun shines,
And even when it rains.
Whatever the situation, Lord,
You Love me just the same.

You've declared that my latter days,
Would better than the rest.
I'm holding to Your promises,
I'm going to do my best.

I'm living my blessed life,
This race has just begun.
Your mercy, love and grace,
Has prepped me for this run.

I'm Living My Blessed Life,
Thanks God for all You do.
I'm Living My Blessed Life.
I owe it all to you.

God Has His Hands on You

When things get a little tough, it's life, they always do.
You will meet these trials, you will see it through,
God has His hands on you.

You don't just talk the talk, we see God lives in you.
You take care of others, you share God's love,
God has His hands on you.

You're always there to help, no matter what it is.
You go over and beyond the call to help others,
God has His hands on you.

You did whatever we asked you, did it with a smile.
You persevered through disappointments.
God has His hands on you.

You do all of this for others, that's just what you do.
In your DNA there's peace and joy,
God has His hands on you.

You will reap what you sow, God said in his word.
You've been a blessing to others,
God has His hands on you.

Your time has come to let God, He takes care of His own.
He blessed you to be a blessing,
God has His hands on you.

Where Were You, God?

Where Were You, God,
When he got shot and died in my arms?
How did You allow this to happen?
He had never done any harm.

Where Were You, God,
When she got sick and was in bed?
You have the power to heal.
Yet death raised its terminal head.

Where Were You, God?
I was losing faith and hope.
I was trying to find consolation.
Trying to find a way to cope.

Where Were You, God?
We've always praised your name.
We're not supposed to have this heartache.
Just wealth, fortune and fame.

Where Were You, God?
Thanks for Your mercy and grace.
You brought me through the tough times.
When death stared me in the face?

Where Were You, God?
You were with me all the time.
Nurtured me and strengthened me.
When I thought I was losing my mind.

Where Were You, God?
It's a part of your divine plan.
If I just learn to accept Your will,
It will make me a wiser man.

Where Were You, God?
When life challenges passed my way?
Thank You for love and protection.
They came to pass and not to stay.

Where Were You, God?
You're always there with me.
I have to trust and believe.
And one day Your face I'll see.

I Remember You, Love, in My Prayers

Every night before I go to sleep,

I pray and cast all of my cares.

I never cease thinking of you,

I Remember You, Love, in My Prayers.

I pray for protection and guidance,

And thank God for all that He shares.

For hope, peace, joy, and love.

I Remember You, Love, in My Prayers.

I ask for forgiveness and discernment,

The favor He grants me is there.

I'm grateful for the blessings that He's given me.

I Remember You, Love, In My Prayers.

Our families and loved ones are covered.

For Heaven, we pray they're prepared.

I'm praying for prosperity for everyone.

As I Remember You, Love, In My Prayers.

Just Believe

Sometimes the hills seem too high to climb,
But don't you be deceived.
You can conquer every challenge,
If you Just Believe.

I've had many dreams and goals,
I thought I couldn't achieve.
I prayed and stayed the course,
And, yes, I Just Believe.

I was lost and burdened down,
No hope to retrieve.
Nothing to keep me from falling,
But yet I Just Believe.

Then I found a risen Savior,
His love I did receive.
He gave me hope and peace,
And a reason to Just Believe.

I now can do all things,
As far as I can perceive.
There are no limits or boundaries,
Because I Just Believe.

Nothing Is Too Hard For God

In life, there will be obstacles
That we can't seem to solve,
But if we just let God,
He will always get involved.

He will provide your every need.
He will even protect your heart.
We just have to remember one thing,
There's Nothing Too Hard For God.

You are such a blessing to others.
You are on God's to-do list today.
He knows just what you need.
He hears you when you pray.

God has a plan for you,
And the doctor has his part.
God will make sure he gets it done.
There's Nothing Too Hard For God.

So now it's time to let God,
He's been with you from the start.
He always takes care of His own,
And There's Nothing Too Hard For God.

A Baby is Born

Who would have thought a Baby would come
To save this world from sin?
He came and showed us how to love,
And this is how His story would begin.

Mary would be chosen as His mother,
Joseph chose this virgin for his wife.
How could this virtuous woman have a baby?
Unless God chose her to give life.

He would be born in Bethlehem in a manger,
And wrapped in swaddling clothes to begin.
Born in a field with the cattle,
Because there was no room at the inn.

The wise men traveled from afar,
Traveling by night and by day.
They were guided by a star in the sky,
Which would show them exactly where He lay.

They would greet Him with praises and gifts.
They knew that the Messiah was now born.
Greeted by the angels to confirm.
Don't return to King Herrod for his scorn.

This Baby would grow up and bring us hope,
Allow us all to be born again.
Who would have thought a Baby would come?
And be the one to save us from our sins?

This Baby's name is Jesus. He's our Savior,
In His name, there is power to cleanse your sin.
Glory to God in the highest,
And on earth peace, goodwill toward men.

Do Your Best,
and God Will Handle the Rest

When the table is stacked against you,
there's no reason to drop your head.
Get on your knees, do your best,
and God will handle the rest.

The challenges that confront you
will draw you closer to Him.
Trust in your faith, do your best,
and God will handle the rest.

For if you just trust in Him, and pray
His will be done,
He takes care of you.
Do your best, and God will handle the rest.

There is no situation or problem
that He's not aware.
He is the Creator, do your best,
and God will handle the rest.

He doesn't always give you
what you think you want.
He has a plan.
Do your best, and God will handle the rest.

He doesn't make mistakes,
and He can never fail.
It works in your favor.
Do your best, and God will handle the rest.

He knows His plan for you, the things you cannot see.
Trust and obey, Do your best,
and God will handle the rest.

Let go and let God handle it,
He's working it out for you.
His plans are to prosper you.
Do your best, and God will handle the rest.

I'm glad I have a God who is looking out for me.
He's got my back, I'll do my best,
and He will handle the rest.

Love Is

Love is a feeling that's so very special.

It's not jealous or bold.

It brings relationships together,

To have and to hold.

Love is patient, and love is kind,

It does not envy nor does it boast.

It allows you to celebrate and appreciate,

The ones you love the most.

Love is not self-seeking and does not dishonor,

It keeps no record of wrong.

Love is what love does,

Keeps your heart beating strong.

Love does not rejoice in evil and always protects,

Always trusts and never fails.

Always hopes and perseveres,

The truth is where love dwells.

Now that we know how God wants us to Love,

Let's choose to stand and agree.

To share this unstoppable love with all,

Is as blessed as it can be.

A Mother's Love

A Mother's Love prepares and protects. It's a tough-love
that is hard to describe.
It loves you whether you're wrong or right. It's a love that
will never be denied.

A Mother's Love helps and encourages. It gives you the faith
that you need to proceed.
To make a jagged edge straight and a heavy burden light,
A Mother's Love is all you need.

A Mothers Love nurtures and provides. It gets you ready for
the journey that's taking place.
There's no measure that A Mother's Love wouldn't go
through to see a big smile on your face.

A Mother's Love prays and gives us peace, when it seems
like all hope here is gone. It picks up the pieces and cleans up
the bruises and gives you the strength that you need to go on.

A Mother's Love for her child is unconditional. There's
nothing that will ever cause it to fade.
We will forever thank God for our Momma. A Mother's
Love is truly heaven made.

A Mother's Love is pure, and it's of God. We know the
blessings that we share come from above. We praise Your
name and thank You Lord for blessing us, and showering us
with favor...A Mother's Love.

It's A New Year

It's a New Year, and we all have a new plan. Our goal is to get better, stand together hand in hand.

I will treat people right, be a good mom or great dad. I will stick to my diet and the workout plan I had.

These resolutions are good, just know when you start, you have to be committed and determined in your heart.

When we make emotional declarations, those dreams fade away. When we declare in our hearts, we can start them today.

To make a change in me first, and move to the rest. Put God at the forefront, so that we get your best.

I can do all things through Christ, in His word we can trust. To start every day with Him is an absolute must.

Your new year is bright, your plan is intact. And when you slip, you won't fall, because God has your back.

Your life is all different, you're restored and anew. This is what happens when you let God do what He do.

Start the New Year with God. A little faith is all you need. Watch the transformation that happens, when He plants His seed.

A New Year and a new life is all at your hand. All you have to do, is put your trust in the Man.

I Thank God for You

I'm just sitting here thinking
About the special things in my life.
You were always there for me,
In the good times and through the strife.

You've always stood beside me,
And helped me to pull it through.
You held my hand and hug my neck.
I Thank God For You.

When I needed someone to talk to,
You listened without a doubt.
And when I had a problem to solve,
You helped me figure it out.

When I needed to make a decision,
I didn't know where to go.
You always had the best advice,
You helped me learn and grow.

When I needed to feel special,
You were the very best.
It seems God sent you straight to me,
You always passed that test.

There has been nothing that I needed,
That you couldn't help me through.
My guardian angel from above,
God gave me His best with YOU.

My sweet Aunt, my mother, my hope, my friend,
I'll always love and appreciate you.
My faith, my joy, my determination,
In you, I can always depend.

I thank our Lord and Savior,
For blessing my life with you.
God molded you with his holy hands,
I Thank God For You!

I just want you to know how much,
I appreciate your precious love.
You prayed for me, you protected me,
Just as God does from up above.

I love you to the moon and back,
You're eternally in my heart.
You are absolutely amazing, love,
You are where my blessings start.

So let me show my gratitude,
And give you what you're due.
You can never imagine how much I love you,
I truly Thank God For you.

Inspired by Family

Inspired by Family

Family: The village of people that is responsible for the way you think, act and behave. My family's influence in my life is the most important reason I am who I am.

I have a rather large and loving family. My mother was the fifth of nine siblings. My grandparents' house was always full of children, as they also raised at least 13 of their grandchildren. On some occasion, I have slept over at six of the eight of my mother's siblings' homes. The Stevenson family is bonded by love and togetherness. Our family's faith and commitment to God is what keeps us inseparable. Not perfect by any means, but solid, authentic and real.

I have to mention my grandparents' names, Hattie Mae and Mason Stevenson, for they provided the foundation of nurturing, caretaking, faith, hope, progress, education and love that is still prevalent in our family today. I had the privilege of spending all of my youth with my grandparents. We had a little space with a lot of love. At any time there could be up to 13 family members who lived in this three bedroom house at one time. Sounds like a lot, but we were always comfortable, and we didn't mind being together. We were raised in the church. We were sent to school to do our best, and we were encouraged to continue with our education after high school.

Growing up, I was surrounded by my favorite cousins that I loved so much. We played football and baseball together, cried and prayed together. We grew up more like brothers and sisters than cousins. The cousin that I was closest to died in my arms with five bullet holes in his chest, due to a lack of gun control and drugs. I'm dedicating this book to him. It is this family that motivates me, influences me, supports me and prays for me every day. The love and experiences in my FAMILY inspired me to write the poems in the following section.

Our Family

Our family is extraordinary.
We were created through love and prayer.
The offspring of Mom and Dad,
And Jesus was always there.

Our family has been tested,
Through generations of joy and pain.
The love of Momma and Daddy,
Have always remained the same.

Our family is strongly protected.
With patience and love for all.
The nurturing that they provided,
Still, today stands tall.

Our family is highly favored.
God's presence was always near.
The example they provided us,
Still, fills our hearts with cheer.

Our family is Spirit-led.
Guided by faith and trust.
Keeping their favored spirit alive,
Is something that we must.

Our family is filled with love.
Blessed with two of the best.
Momma and Daddy's hope for us,
We can't ever let it rest.

Our family is one of faith,
And we're back together again.
The joy that we got from them both,
Shall never, ever end.

Our family is not broken.
We have the ties that bind.
The union of our parents,
Have stood the test of time.

Our family has a mission,
To commit to this loving brand.
The sacrifices of our mom and dad,
Spread it throughout the land.

Real Love

Every special song that I hear makes me think of you.
They remind me of all the things that I thought we'd get to do.
I know that with you, I enjoy all of the special things.
And bring to realization, the joy that Real Love brings.

Whether we are sitting around the table, or hanging in a room,
The presence of this Real Love always seems to loom.
How do you know it's real? That's what they might say.
They didn't feel my heart when it fluttered the other day.

Do not know the place, nor can I remember the time,
All I know is that you are ever present, always on my mind.
When I wake up in the morning, or before I go to bed,
This Real Love stays constantly, consistently in my head.

This Real Love has survived the distance that time alone may bring,
And the love that is between us is such a beautiful thing.
This relationship is an understanding between two friends.
And the love, respect, and passion that we see will never end.

Real love is present here. I can see it in your eyes.
It has never lost its way but has put up a great disguise.
This Real Love has never left, and I hope it's here to stay,
And this very true Real Love, still takes my breath away.

FAMILY

A family is a group of kin.
That doesn't mean we are alike.
We share a common thread, some moral values.
And somewhat a common plight.

We share the same blood,
There is none like our brand.
And in the time of need and strife,
We always lend a hand.

We share the same parents.
They helped us pave the way.
We share the same forgiving heart.
They showed us how to pray.

We share the same siblings,
And we have quite a few.
We cried together and played together,
And whatever else we could do.

We share a common name,
The brand we share was born.
Built on love and hope,
We weathered through the storm.

We share a common mission
To make our parents proud.
They loved, provided and nurtured us.
Their actions spoke so loud.

We share the same loving God.
He hears us when we pray.
He's blessed us and anointed us,
And brought us from a mighty long way.

We share this opportunity,
He's spared us another day.
We are still going strong,
And touching lives along the way.

Don't Waste Another Day

Take the time to smell the roses.
Don't turn and walk away.
The time we have is precious.
Don't Waste Another day.
Special moments that we've shared
are stored and locked away.
We'll bring them out and remember
to savor another day.
Don't take our relationship for granted.
This love is true and real.
And there is no mistaking what we believe and feel.
I'm glad that God allowed you to see me through.
And I want you to know that
I'm always here for YOU.
The days are way too short,
the nights much too long.
With the passing of each day, keep it going strong.
This is the day, so let's rejoice in the love we share.
And know that without a doubt
that we love and care.
A test of this love, the things we do and say.
Time is of the essence.
Don't Waste another Day.

Celebrating YOU

Celebrating You,
The person of our dreams.
Since the day we met,
It's been perfect for us, it seems.
Celebrating You,
Because we love to see you smile.
You have that awesome pedigree,
A strong, and caring style.
Celebrating You,
You deserve all of this and more.
You give so much of yourself,
Never closing any door.
Celebrating You,
You make others fill with cheer.
Always giving from your heart,
Forever oh, so dear.
Celebrating You,
You bring joy to all.
Whenever there's a need,
You answer every call.
Celebrating You,
Enjoy your special day.
It's time to be celebrated,
In each and every way.

JOYCE

You came to us, and you judged us not.
We accepted you into our life.
You're such an awesome sister, aunt, and member of
this family,
And to Jerome a virtuous wife.

You've served our family in every capacity.
You've stepped out and led the way.
You've shown us a perfect example of love,
And you've done it on any given day.

Our parents loved and cherished you Mrs. Stevenson,
Joyce, as daddy would say, "That's my girl."
Susie said, "Hattie Mae was her Naomi and she...was
her Ruth,"
The most faithful daughter-in-law in the world.

This family is blessed with an extraordinary gift.
Joyce, you're always giving from the heart.
You are someone dear to every family member here.
Whatever the role, you've played your part.

We appreciate your love and dedication.
We are celebrating you today.
Give you your flowers while you yet live.
We Love You Dearly, as you always say.

In-law, that's not a just title for you.
Just love without fortune or fame.
FAMILY you are to us, Carlotta Joyce,
And we thank God in Jesus' name.

We've learned that you don't have to share the
same blood,
For you to be Family and a friend.
You've rewritten the book on loving thy neighbor.
You're not just Family, you're kin.

I Love You

These three words are powerful,

We hear them every day.

They mean that without a doubt,

My heart is with you to stay.

I Love You has a meaning,

That encompasses the heart and soul,

And they go beyond measure,

More precious than diamonds and gold.

They're the reason that when I see you,

My heart skips a beat.

And the reason when we're together,

I always reach my peak.

Taller than the highest mountain,

I Love you makes me know,

I'm not acting off of emotions,

Or putting on a show.

The best way to explain I Love You,

MAGIC has to be real.

The only word that I could think of,

To explain the way I feel.

So Easy To Love

So Easy to Love,
Always here when there's a need.
Loving, caring and sharing,
The authentic servant's creed.

So Easy to Love,
And no matter where you are.
You stick out amongst the rest,
Outshining the brightest star.

So Easy to Love,
We can trust and depend on you.
Failing is not an option,
When you do things like you do.

So Easy to Love,
You have that special gift.
To Teach, Motivate, and Challenge,
Encourage and Uplift.

So Easy to Love,
Because you serve with pride.
You give God all the glory.
Your steps, He orders and guides.

So Easy to Love,
And I know that in the end,
A love that's easy to love,
Will always be my friend.

So Easy to Love,
Your passion always shines through.
You are to be celebrated,
Appreciated for all you do.

Smile

There's one thing that I like to see,
It's like you're putting on a show.
All I know is when you smile,
Makes my heart glow.

Of my choice of your expressions,
That's the one that I choose.
Your smile just makes me feel,
There's no way that I can lose.

I like to do the things,
To put a smile upon your face.
It leaves a permanent impression,
That can never be erased.

The smile on your face,
Is a reflection of your heart.
The love and joy that it portrays,
The intent right from the start.

If I could make you happy,
Your smile won't go away.
As long as I am here for you,
That Smile is there to stay.

To Celebrate You

To Celebrate You, and your
years upon this land,
We kindly take your mission, to
simply lend a hand.
You're always serving others, a
helping hand to all.
When there is a need to serve,
you answer every call.

To Celebrate You, your passion
for people is true.
We appreciate your service and
all that you do.
We celebrate the cause, your
date of birth is near.
Time to show appreciation,
Happy Birthday Dear.

The Love of My Life

The love of my life,
Baby, that's who you are.
The queen of my castle,
My beautiful shining star.

There is no other person,
That can ever take your place.
You were sent to me from Heaven,
My sweet, saving grace.

I thank God for the woman
That He made just for me.
And I made a choice,
The best husband I'd be.

You are bone of my bone,
My love for you is true.
And we are but one,
And I'm lost without you.

We are on a journey,
That will last an entire life.
I'll honor, love, protect
And respect you, my wife.

I know I'm not perfect,
But I am fair and true.
And there is nothing in this world,
That I wouldn't do for you.

So sit back and hold on,
We're blessed by the Savior.
He gives more than we ask,
He provides us His favor.

So the blessings we share,
They come straight from above.
And you have my heart,
My unconditional love.

The love of my life,
He blessed me with you.
We are in this together,
It's what love made us do.

No thief alive,
Can steal what we share.
For as long as there's you,
I'll always be there.

The mother to my kids,
You're my beautiful wife.
You're my eternal mate,
And the love of my life.

So to ensure that I'm yours,
I asked for your hand.
I'm with you forever,
And that's all in God's plan.

No reason to ever doubt,
He's great and divine.
We're together forever,
Until the end of all time.

The Best Day of My Life
A Letter To My Son

Have you ever had a day that you didn't want to leave?

The Best Day of My Life, you just wouldn't believe.

God gave me a son and gave him all to me.

I made my God a promise, the best father I would be.

He was everything I prayed for, and even better than that.

A loving smile, a sweet spirit, and that's of God, a fact.

I want to be there for him, through the good and the bad.

And let him know he's the best son that a man has ever had.

God gave His Son Jesus, so that me and mine could live.

That's the ultimate sacrifice, my son, I could not give.

I thank my Lord and Savior, for blessing me with you.

I ask for love and guidance, to help us see it through.

I've had some pretty good days. Some days I won't forget.

But there is only one day, that's truly too legit.

Not winning the championships,

or even the marrying of my wife.

The day my son was born, was The Best Day of My Life.

Proud to be Your Pop
A Note To My Daughter, My Friend

I came into your life a stranger, a totally different world.

We hit it off from the start, such a cute and silly girl.

I have watched you grow and learn, some bumps along the way.

You didn't let them get you down, you got better every day.

This journey has just begun and it will never stop.

Just wanted you to know that I'm proud to be your pop.

I've watched you become a young lady, a style of your own.

Classy and beautiful, and bad to the bone.

Studious and sophisticated, a girl that's smart and strong.

Don't let this makeup fool you, I'll put you where you belong.

Your competitive nature and loving spirit, the cream of the crop.

I'm such a lucky guy and I'm proud to be your pop.

As life goes on, time passes, just know that I am here.

I thank God for our relationship, I love you, oh so dear.

Continue to strive and work hard, your goal is to be the best.

And there is no stopping you, you will outwork all the rest.

Your dreams, your goals and work ethic, will take you to the top.

I am blessed to have as a daughter, I'm proud to be your pop.

Your Best

You have studied all you can,
You're prepared for the test.
Nothing for you to worry about,
Because you've done your best.

There are times when your best,
It just don't get it done.
Good, better, best are choices,
You've done your best, so run.

If you've done your best,
You should really feel good.
You've prepared the proper way,
Just the way you should.

So hold your head up high,
Don't forget to stick out your chest.
Results don't always tell,
Whether or not you've done your best.

YOU

When we were feeling down
And thought that all was up,
You told us to keep working and praying,
That God would fill the cup.

When we needed advice and comfort,
You gave us what we needed.
We have a chance to share our gifts,
You've been a friend indeed.

When we needed love and confidence,
Without judging, you took our hand.
Told us to have some patience,
You helped us understand.

When we thought that we were falling,
You showed us how to stand strong.
And when we needed a shoulder to cry on,
You never left us alone.

When we thought that we were good,
You showed us how to be the best.
You said live life abundantly,
And don't ever have regrets.

When everything was going wrong,
And you were hurting too,
You kept it all together,
And helped us see it through.

So we all came to support
And express our love for you.
You keep all of us alive,
That's just what you do.

So now we want to encourage you,
You still get it right.
Keep praying, teaching and sharing God's love.
You are shining bright.

All of the other families
Can experience the love we know.
You've always sacrificed yourself,
To help all others grow.

You do all of this because
You serve an AWESOME God.
You're appreciated for your service.
You have a champion's heart.

Time Just Don't Wait

I wish I could see all of you right now,

Let's not wait too late.

Time will come and time will go,

Time Just Don't Wait.

"I wish I was," "I wish I did,"

Are words to which we all can relate.

Let us do, and yes I did,

Because Time Just Don't Wait.

Our loved ones that have gone before,

Did not decide their fate.

Let's do what we can while we are here,

Time Just Don't Wait.

Just to see your smile and hear your voice,

That would be so great.

Don't know the next time our paths may cross,

Because Time Just Don't Wait.

Just You

It's Just You
Who makes all of my cloudy skies blue.
Your touch and your smile
Allow the sun to shine through.

It's Just You
Who makes my darkest paths bright.
Your listening ear and loving smile,
Makes everything alright.

It's Just You
When I feel everything's going wrong.
You say the words I like to hear,
It keeps me going strong.

It's Just You
When I feel like things are going to end.
You say the words to encourage
And I brighten up again.

It's Just You
Who allows me to just go be me.
And when I feel that's not enough,
You encourage me to be free.

It's Just You
Who tells me not to ever give in.
And I know how it feels
To have a partner and a friend.

It's Just You
Who God put in my life just for me.
You're my rock and my strength,
Here for me eternally.

When You Love Like This

When you love like this,
It's a magic that fills the air.
It captures your mind and heart,
You know you really care.

There is nothing that's too big,
Nor a task that's too small.
To make your heart happy,
For you, no task too tall.

To capture that special moment,
Happiness overtakes the heart.
To get to that secret place,
Where loving really starts.

When you love like this,
Can't explain the way you feel.
You have to be in the moment,
Or you won't believe it's real.

The impossible come to life,
Who believes in fairytales?
To be free to love and be yourself,
Love always will prevail.

When you love like this,
Your heart begins to melt.
And you know without a doubt,
It's the best feeling you've ever felt.

You will feel like all is good,
This tender love and care.
With each and every moment,
Embrace the love you share.

When you love like this,
You know when it begins.
You have learned how to love.
Don't ever let it end.

True Love is Forever

Time passes as it always does,
People come, and they will go.
True Love is Forever.
In due time you will know.

It might disappear,
You try to let it go.
True Love is Forever,
In time, it will only grow.

The chance comes to show your love,
Release the feelings that you hide.
True Love Is Forever,
You've hidden them all along inside.

A passionate, real relationship,
Two hearts that beat as one.
True Love Last Forever,
Until all is said and done.

Celebrated and respected,
Honored to be in love.
A true love that is Forever,
Could only come from above.

Inspired by Friends

Inspired by Friends

Friends: the group of individuals who I've associated with and that I have built a relationship with over a period of time. These relationships, whether new or old, have inspired me to write some of my most innovative work. I may not know the subject to whom I'm writing while doing a piece for a friend, so I have to try and put myself in that specific situation. In most cases, I ask that they only furnish me with a title and I pray and allow God to lead me in writing. Some want to convey a message to a special friend, while others may want to say "I love you" to their spouse. I get enjoyment in helping to put a smile on others' faces.

I have different levels of friendship. I have lifelong friends. These are friends that grew up in the same community and that I've known since adolescence years. I have high school friends that I love dearly. These high school friends share with me some of the most impactful moments of my life. My high school years were fun and exciting. I'm forever grateful to all of my classmates, and I will always cherish the memories we created. I have college friends, most of which are my fraternity brothers. I stayed in my home state to go to college, so a lot of my high school friends went to college in close vicinity. Lastly, I have friends that I have picked up along the way as I have taught in two different states and traveled to many cities. These relationships were developed in a short period of time, but have been most impactful in my quest to publish a book. The friendships along the way are the most active because these are the people that I get to share my poetry with on almost a daily basis. These friends along with a few others are always encouraging me to publish so that these works can be shared with others. I am grateful that some friends have encouraged me to write poems, and others have convinced me to share what I've written.

And for this, FRIENDS, I can say thank you for your encouragement and inspiration for the following section of poems.

Good Luck, My Friend

In life, we sometimes make a change,
To leave or stay the same.
We have to go where God will lead,
Even though it brings some pain.

He will never leave nor forsake you.
He's been tried, tested and true.
He's prepared you for this very day,
And I know He'll see you through.

We will miss your presence around here,
You helped all of us grow each day.
I know you will make others dreams come true,
And help show them the way.

You always had a listening ear.
Your mission was to be the best.
You took great pride in getting it done,
And did it better than all of the rest.

You cherished the people with whom you worked,
On you, we could depend.
You planned you prepared, you guided,
And you grinded to the end.

One day I hope that you look back
On the people that you've served.
And I know that they appreciate you.
You gave them more than they deserved.

The late-night study hall on Sundays.
The team meetings each week.
The sleepless nights during finals.
The waking them from their sleep.

There was no task too big or one too small,
That you would not take charge.
No task that you wouldn't confront,
No matter how small or large.

Our family won't ever forget,
All you did to help others grow.
We appreciate all of your dedication,
More than you could know.

You won't easily be replaced.
The standard you help set will stand.
We will keep your champion spirit alive,
And stay the best in all the land.

As you go back home to the family,
And your stint here comes to an end,
We wish you all the best,
Good luck to you, my friend.

The Beast in Me

Before I hit the bed each night,
You know I bow my head.
Give thanks to the Almighty,
For the Beast in me He bred.

For I would not have this attitude,
Basketball wouldn't be the same.
The Beast in Me wouldn't live,
If God hadn't done His thang.

So I will forever be thankful,
And give honor and praises to God.
I'll show the Beast inside of me,
That we must do our part.

When we get up in the morning,
And before we lace up these sneaks.
I'll pray that God prepares us,
To help us reach our peaks.

God gives us the endurance to finish,
Supply us all of our needs.
Tame the Beast within me,
To always plant Your seeds.

It's time to go to work,
We appreciate all God's done.
Me and the Beast inside of Me,
On the court for Him, we run.

You Are So Beautiful

You are so beautiful, your eyes tell a tale.
They keep me hypnotized, they put me in a spell.
The beauty that you portray
goes more profound than the skin.
Your pretty brown frame,
from beginning to the end.

Your sweet and sexy lips,
an accent to your smile.
That swaggy natural hair,
your stunning natural style.
The way you dress is flawless,
your smile is the best.
The features of your face,
are better than all the rest.

I can go on and on about how beautiful you look.

It would take a lifetime, I could write a book.
You are so beautiful, I'll sum it up this way.
The classy, sexy style brightens up my day.

To add to that awesomeness,
a sense of humor and grace.
It keeps me in a trance, in another time and place.
Your beauty is more than skin deep,
a glamour from within.
Glad to know you,
and to have you as my friend.

The Sweetest Girl I Know

She walks around with a beautiful smile.
It makes her personality glow.
She has a charming style with grace.
She's the sweetest girl I know.

She takes care of all with love and care,
And never gets too high or low.
She makes even the toughest task seem small.
She's the sweetest girl I know.

She has the style that every woman wants.
Sensational, and has a heart that glows.
So special, she is to me.
She's the sweetest girl I know.

Quiet confidence is what she portrays,
And when she dances, she takes over the floor.
She's always better than the best,
And she's the sweetest girl I know.

There for You

Your journey is just beginning,
your eyes are on the prize.
You're getting yourself prepared,
getting ready for the ride.
You can't do this alone, you need some help you know.
You can all be successful, if you help each other grow.
You need a little faith, to help you get a start.
You'll need some joy and love, just store them in your heart.
The foundation is laid, your mission for you to be.
God gave you a vision, that no one else can see.
You must trust and depend, that He will see you through.
Whatever test may come your way,
He's always there for you.
Determination is a must when obstacles get in the way.
You'll need some strength and patience
to get you through the day.
Jealousy is around the corner, it's trying to hold you back.
Family and friends alike, so keep some prayer intact.
And just when everything's ok, you start to see the light.
That old pessimistic spirit will start to take its plight.
This is when the God you serve, is at His very best.
You have to call upon His name, to put Him to the test.
The sun can't always shine, without a little rain.
And you wouldn't know how great would feel,
without a little pain.
All you need to know right now, is God is there for you.
Success is on the other side, I pray you make it through.

Who Am I

Who am I?
Do I even want to know?
Does the way that I think,
Help me learn and grow?
Do I have to analyze it?
Or am I hard and abstract?
I sometimes can create it,
And sometimes I use the facts.
I can communicate at all times,
My social skills are great.
You can give me a list of things to do,
But I'm better when I create.
I like to build relationships,
My love and trust are true.
I'll give everyone a chance,
I'll give my best to you.
I'm a very aggressive person,
About something that I care about,
But if your topic is of no concern to me,
I'll be as quiet as a mouse.
I'll do whatever you want me to do,
To put a smile on your face.

And if you only choose to start,
I'll help you finish the race.
My ways are not my ways,
I was sent to help and serve.
Just be loyal and straight-forward with me,
I don't adjust well to a curve.
Maybe the way that I think,
Controls the way that I behave.
Can I make everyone happy?
That is what I really crave.
If you allow me to be myself,
I want to connect with you.
Helping and serving others,
Is what God sent me to do.
The way that we behave and think,
Is a mystery to us no more.
Open up your mind and heart,
And unlock this very door.
Who Am I?
Now I think I know.
But the mystery is still unsolved,
If you continue to learn and grow.

You Get It Done

There are some folks in life who try to do things right.

They challenge themselves to be the best,

every day and night.

Whether being a loving person

or even when you're not so fun,

Somehow and some way, you seem to Get it Done.

You are committed to the important things,

and give it all you got.

We always get your very best, whether we like it or not.

A strong, positive influence, a hard-worker indeed.

When God made you, He made the rarest breed.

The people in your life that God gave you to lead,

Are held to the highest standard, and prepared to succeed.

There is no other person, who works as hard as you.

Working hard with pride and passion, that's what you do.

When the final score is settled, and last race is run,

I can depend on you, because You Get it Done.

Tough but compassionate, hard but fair and true,

You Get it Done, we get the best from you.

Direction

A new day has dawned, it's my time to shine,
To prepare, it's going to be real.
My time has come, my day to conquer,
I have a challenge and role to fill.

God direct my path, I'm ready to grow.
I'll be the example You need me to be.
Give me the strength to lead by example,
It must first all begin with me.

As I grow each day, I'm depending on you,
To give us the ingredients that we need.
The grit to fight through the toughest of times,
As You plan our foundation to succeed.

I need your direction, I desire to soar.
My aim is to train to be the best.
Whatever it is, that I need to do,
To be better than all of the rest.

Stand up and be counted, I'm committed,
I'm ready to run and to win.
The Direction I go and the will to persevere,
I'm ready to fight 'til the end.

Poised For Progress

As the passing of each hour, time passes like a blur.
The decisions we make affect the future,
however it may occur.
I'm Poised for Progress. I'll take a stance.
No pressure to withstand.
I'm built for this.
I represent the best in all of the land.

No need to waste your time to ponder,
look me in the eye.
Tell me that I'm not Poised for Progress,
ask no reasons why.
I'll serve this great mission,
with integrity, style, and grace.
I'm Poised for Progress, I am prepared to win this race.

So if you see me and I'm not on point,
know I'm on my way.
Poised for greatness, keep my composure,
prepared to attack and slay.
My character is unblemished,
I'm focused and won't be denied.
There's no way that I will fail, with God by my side.

It Just Feels Right

Only time will tell if it's right or wrong.
Do you spend special time together,
or leave each other alone.
This relationship is a mystery.
Control is out of sight.
A fluttering heart, some sweaty hands,
it just feels right.
You will analyze the situation,
of course, you'll do what's right.
Follow the paths of your hearts,
or this feeling should you fight.
Your past is forever present,
you've never let it go.
Don't want to erase the memories that
cause your hearts to glow.
Your analytical self tells you,
that you just might.
But your conceptual heart tells you,
It Just Feels Right.

What Color?

What color?
The person that comes to lend a hand.
Does it matter?
If they care or if they understand.
A child doesn't judge people on color, you see.
It doesn't matter whether or not
you're the same color as me.
God made all His creation,
and He said it was good.
Did he mention a color?
Use His example, we should.
The dream is still alive
and should come from within.
The content of my character,
not the color of my skin.
What color are you? Is it the color of love?
Let's use the example that was sent from above.
What color?
To treat everyone the way that God treats you.
To love and forgive should be easy for us to do.

How do you make me feel?
Does it depend on my shade?
And the color of my skin,
shouldn't make you afraid.
What color?
All that's in Heaven's hands shall be right.
Brothers and sisters praising,
no color is in sight.
What color?
Our aim here on earth should be,
To love and respect all, the truth sets us free.
What color?
On God, we should all still depend.
His perfect love is the same
with the differences of skin.
Tone, shade or color is not where it begins.
But we shall all learn to live
with the skin that we're in.
Do a self-evaluation, watch the kids,
they will show.
How do you treat me and make me feel?
What color, you know?

Because I Luv You

Because I luv you, you became my friend.
Stayed through the stormy weather,
Through the thick and through the thin.

Because I luv you, I will stand by your side.
I appreciate your love and,
with you I'll always ride.

Because I luv you,
I will continue to run this race.
We're in this special season of our life,
Because of God's mercy and His grace.

Because I luv you,
I'm yours for forevermore.
And I am so excited, for the future,
what's in store.

Now, don't think I'm getting soft.
Still got my knife and gun.
But because I luv ya dude,
I'll let you to have some fun.

My Love

My love for you is strong and true,
It removes all of my doubt.
I can't keep it to myself,
I have to let it out.

My love for you gives me peace,
I'll love you until the end.
Appreciative of this relationship,
You'll always have a friend.

My love I'm ever grateful,
You give me what I need.
My love has ignited a fire,
And planted a lifelong seed.

And when my love long for comfort,
The way is bright and clear.
It shows up and lead the way.
My love, we share, is dear.

His Journey

His Journey had to start somewhere,
Who'd know when it began?
That God was building a mighty empire,
With His most impactful men.

All brought together by the same guy,
With a platform was to serve and praise God.
Tim Maloney, you stepped out on faith.
His Journey might have seemed so hard.

Life comes with some very big challenges,
Lord, this is what I want to do.
But to make my Heavenly Father proud,
I want it to be pleasing with You.

His love, His mercy and His grace,
During my attack was all that I need.
He protected me from the enemy,
So I could continue planting His seed.

Thanks Lord for the influence you've given me.
Thanks for allowing me to play a part.
Thanks for the road I had to travel.
Thanks for the extra artery on my heart.

You knew from the day of my birth,
The ambitious soldier that I would be.
Thanks for sending me Joanne,
To go on His Journey with me.

The people that you put in my life,
Thomas, Earnest, Teddy, Ryan and the rest,
God grant me Your Heavenly Power,
So I can give to ALL my best.

In His Journey we travel many miles,
To get to wherever we belong.
Just know that wherever God leads us,
Is a place we can always call home.

Inspired by Football

Inspired by Football

Football is a popular game that is played by a team. The team members are instructed by older individuals called coaches. There is an audience that cheers on the team as they compete against each other, and we refer to them as fans. Well, for all of my life, football has been an important part of it, as a player, coach or as a fan. From the moment that I started playing football at the age of 6 until now, the game of football has taught me some valuable lessons. I have also learned some lessons from the players I've coached, and I have gained some great knowledge from other coaches I've worked with in the business. The relationships you build along the way are bonds that you will cherish for the rest of your life.

If you learn to respect the game, the game will be good to you. The rules are designed to make sure everyone has an equal chance at winning on an even playing field. There are also rules designed for the safety of the players playing the game. When done right, football is a tough game, but it's fun and fair.

To win in this game, you must first have good players. The team with the most discipline and the endurance to finish usually wins when everything else is equal. So this game teaches you how to compete on a team. You have to be tough and have good leadership to reach a level to attain a competitive edge. A game plan has to be designed and executed to get to where you have success consistently. There is communication going on between coaches and coaches, and coaches and players at the same time. In the midst of all of that chaos, the players have to keep their composure and get their job done. What do you say to keep them focused and on the task at hand? "Prior preparation prevents piss poor performance." "Work will win when wishing won't." Whatever you do or say, you want your team to respond and perform. What will you say to get the winning edge? What will you do to get the victory? The relationships gained from football and challenges of the game have motivated me to write the poems in the following section.

This Team

Nothing in the world like This Team,

Our priorities are where they belong.

We eat, sleep and pray together,

Our love for each other is strong.

This Team is like a prized fighter,

Preparing for a heavyweight bout.

Patiently and strategically waiting,

For the chance to knock the opposition out.

This Team is like a pack of wild dogs,

That bonded together as one.

Traveling with the same purpose,

One goal, get the job done.

This Team is like an unstoppable train,

Moving at the highest of speeds.

Spreading peace and love,

As they plant a foundation to succeed.

This Team is like an army of brothers,

Highly favored and ready for war.

Protected, prepared and positioned,

To takeover wherever you are.

If you want to be a part of This Team,

Make hard work a part of your plan.

You must hold on to all of God's promise,

And prepare to be the best in the land.

What Football Is To Me

I want to tell you "What Football is To Me."
It's more than just a game you see.
It saved my life, a long time ago.
I was living way too fast from the normal flow.

Doing all the wrong things at 12 was my groove.
I was the man, I thought I was cool.
I started playing real young, I knew X's and O's.
I'd mastered this game, I guess, I suppose.

In the game of life, I was failing a bit.
I knew everything, you couldn't tell me sh--.
And this game that I played all of my life,
Taught me to overcome, all agony and strife.

So, it's the players in the game, that's important to me.
More important than the plan, to win the game you see.
The philosophy is important, your X's and my O's,
But we wouldn't have a chance, without the Jimmies
and Joes.

We won plenty of games as a player and coach. The
championships, the all-star games, the records we broke.
All of these are great but what's there to show,
A ring, a watch, a trophy or so.

We all coach to build a championship team,
Win it all, is every coaches' dream.
But the CHAMPION, the player, has a sound mind.
He makes the right decision, time after time.

Not every player is born as a champion to start,
You must earn their trust, you must win their heart.
They are great athletes, they all have pro dreams.
It is all about self, they weren't born as a team.

This is what football, the game is to me.
To win this player over, to be the best WE, you see.
For if we work together, we can accomplish much more.
Everyone gets rewarded and gets what is in store.

You see I have another Coach, the Savior of men,
And He has the power to cleanse us from sin.
He allows us to have all of these great things,
All the glamour, the limelight, these beautiful rings.

He only requires for us to give back,
Some needy souls, some lives to impact.
To stand up before man and give Him the praise.
Through Him I can do all, is my favorite phrase.

I understand now, what this game made me do,
To give up myself and share me with you.
A fellow coach, a player, staff member or friend,
A prayer, a kind word or time just to spend.

The ultimate success and the greatest of all goals,
Is to share that in Christ, we can be made whole.
The desires of your heart is what He will do,
If you just let the world know, what He's done for you.

See, football has taught me the greater things in life.
How to be a good father and how to treat my wife.
How to deal with the results, when I call a bad play.
How to treat all others, how to kneel and to pray.

Football is a mission that God gave to me,
And for a lot of young men, a father I'd be.
He gave them a football so they could have hope,
From the gangs, bad homes and all of the dope.

Football to me is a way to give back,
To all of those who have fallen, off the right track.
If you just keep on trying and do the best you can do,
Football saved me, I pray something saves you.

Who Am I?

I often sit alone in silence,
And wonder who I am.
Am I who you want me to be,
Or who God says I am.

Can I make the right decisions
of what's best for me to do?
Do I let you influence me to choose what's best for you?

Do I let my light shine and be a vessel for Him to use?
Or will I be a follower, in which the devil will abuse?

Will I allow the lessons I've learned
to help me pave my way?
Or will I listen to my peers and quickly go astray?

Will I be planting seeds of hope as I move
from here to there?
Will I make bad choices
that leaves to hurt and despair?

We all know what to do,
But we don't do it every day.
But we can't control the consequences,
When we slip along the way.

Who am I?
I want to let you know.
Am I for real?
Or am I putting on a show?

Who am I?
Do I really want to know?
The more that I live,
The more I expect to grow.

I'm not a finished product,
I've got you by my side.
If you want what's best for me,
With you, I'll take a ride.

Who will I be?
Should my conscience be my guide?
Will I be my own me?
Or will I let you help me decide?

I'm headed to the top,
I've got all the tools I need.
If I just stick to the plan,
Then I'll live out my creed.

Filthy Physical

The time has now come,
There are decisions you have to make.
Take your time to be in a hurry,
There is so much more at stake.
You are trained to be a CHAMPION,
Every day will be great.
Go fight for what you work for,
The time is now don't wait.
We are Committed and have the Discipline,
That's just how we roll.
We are Bama to the core,
Mind, body, and soul.
Our Effort is relentless,
Our Toughness sets us apart.
The grind is what we thrive on,
We cherish it in our hearts.
PRIDE in how we finish the drill,
The Champions we strive to be.
Built by Bama and the Down for my brother,
Will forever be with me.
The memories and the brotherhood,
Shall never, ever change.
No Excuses, Filthy Physical,
That's how we play the game.

Keys to Success

We have to do things the right way,
if we want to be the best.
We have to take time to study,
if we want to ACE the test.
Going through the motions, won't get you very far.
Challenge yourself to be the best,
so you can raise the bar.

The Keys to Success are simple, we use them every day.
If we make them our daily habits,
we won't stumble along the way.
Be on time and have your supplies,
impress them from the start.
Be attentive and put that phone away,
now that's not very hard.

If you just get involved and participate in the class,
Prepare, present and perform,
just as you do on the grass.
You will perform at the highest level,
and you will do your best.
Success is the byproduct when you do all the rest.

You didn't come here just to play, to WIN is the aim.
On the field and in the classroom,
we have to play the game.
Here are the Keys to Success, try them out and see.
You won't just have a contract,
you'll also have a degree!

Myself

I came into this world all by myself,
And God made it happen this way.
I need to be able to like myself,
Whatever comes, what may.
I need to be able to push myself,
No matter how hard the test.
And know that I would challenge myself,
To always do my best.
When times get tough for myself,
I can't let it get me down.
I gotta be able to pick-up myself,
And get ready for another roun'.
For it is up to me, myself,
To look me in the eye.
And know that I didn't cheat myself,
Because I failed to try.
I give you the best I have, myself,
And be all that I can be.
And always promise to present myself,
The best version I have of me.

Love and Guts

It all began with a choice,
be a part of the special fam.
The best of all of the rest,
with my brothers, here I am.
The early morning summers,
coach built the strongest team.
The offseason in the winter,
to help us reach our dream.
We are building CHAMPIONS here,
with all of the bolts and nuts.
The ingredients that keep us solid,
our TEAM has Love and Guts.
We've done all of the little things right,
kept our hands behind the line.
Finished every drill through the cone,
we always made our time.
This season has not been perfect,
injured soldiers along the way.
Love and Guts and the next man up,
prepare to win today.

We persevered through the tough times,
we're savages, that's all we know.
We lick our wounds, get up and finish,
Learn, prepare and grow.
We won't bend or break, laser-beam focused today.
We won't let our brothers down,
Love and Guts will find a way.
Put me in the game Coach, can't let my brother fall.
Love and Guts on the line, I'll answer the call.
We will never make excuses, we find a way to shine.
Love and Guts will find a way
when it's time to bump and grind.
We have that CHAMPIONS stare,
let's catch that second wind.
Love and Guts for my teammates,
Love and Guts for the WIN!

Patience

Patience, they say, is a virtue.
If you have it, it's good, don't you know.
But if you don't have this special quality,
Then you still have room left to grow.

You may need some time to get better.
You may need to strengthen your mind.
You may need some time to gain knowledge.
You may need to learn how to grind.

Once you have a good dose of Patience,
You'll find out that life's not so bad.
You'll respect all of the hard work,
Receive a joy, like you've never had.

So Lord please give me some Patience.
Help me be the best I can be.
If You just grant me some Patience,
I can be all that's expected of me.

Appreciate the rules of the process,
A plan that will prepare you to win.
Make your dreams a beautiful reality,
Let Patience become your best friend.

Expectations won't be such a headache,
Ambition won't get in the way.
Disappointments won't occur quite as often,
God grant me some Patience today.

It's Not Just All About Me

Life will throw you some twists and some turns,
Just try to be all you can be.
Find a way to give to others,
It's not just all about me.

We have a duty to love and share,
And help them to be all they can be.
We've been blessed to be a blessing,
It's not just all about me.

God wants us all to be cheerful givers,
And help others beyond what they can see.
Challenge them to strive and reach their potential,
It's not just all about me.

If I can just love and help all of God's children,
And we are able to touch and agree.
Attain what it is that they're striving to do,
For it's not just all about me.

To be a good leader and take care of others,
Or motivate them to be the best that they can be.
Be a great example of how to serve others,
It's not just all about me.

Life

Some come into your life and leave without a reason,
Others come and go and only stay for a season.
We never know the answer, but time will reveal,
If the relationship will fade, or if it will last for real.
If you really love something, you can agree to let it go.
With the passing of each moment,
it will cause your love to grow.
Love has no limit, and no distance could ever part.
Time is not a factor, when someone has your heart.
And once they reconnect,
the time that's passed will show,
It's only enriched these feelings,
and caused this love to grow.
You'll remember those days of old,
these emotions that you've hidden inside,
The outburst of what comes next,
a love that's hard to describe.
I can no longer live without you,
I have to feel your touch.
I need you to understand, that I love you very much.
If I would have known then, and listened to my heart,
Who, what, why, when, where,
Sorry, I wasn't so smart.

Finish the Race

It's Our Time to get it done.
At least that's what we say.
Actions speak louder than words,
We gotta win today.

No time to relax,
Winning is all work, but fun.
Gotta get the game plan right,
If we going to get it done.

Tomorrow is not important,
Today we have to shine.
Focus on the task at hand,
And put the past behind.

It's Our Time, that's our cry,
We have to keep the pace.
We have to check our hearts and minds,
We must Finish the Race.

The race don't always go,
To the team that is the best.
But the team that executes,
And show up and pass the test.

We will conquer the challenges.
We gotta get it right.
This team will stick together.
We gonna win tonight.

Snap up that doggone chin straps,
Make sure these cleats are laced.
As a team, we'll come together.
We're gonna Finish the Race.

We will not be the team,
Who just got to the show.
Get ready, here we come.
We're kicking down the door.

Hungry and Determined

I'm hungry and determined,
This is where it all begins.
I have to keep my goals in sight,
To make it to the end.

I'm committed to putting in the work,
I'll do whatever it takes.
Failure is not an option,
When you've seen and know the stakes.

I pray that God protects me,
On this anointed ground I run.
He gave me this game I love to play,
To allow me to have some fun.

I'm hungry and determined,
And I work and grind each day.
I'll run through you, spin and jump over you,
If you get in my way.

I've trained and prepared to win,
I'm following God's Holy plan.
He allowed me a little adversity,
To make me a stronger man.

I'm gonna make it happen,
The truth is what I've heard.
I can do all things through Christ,
God said it in His word.

I'm hungry and determined,
And with God by my side,
I run for Him and feel unstoppable,
In my heart, His word I hide.

So when you see me running touchdowns,
"How he does that," they might say?
I'm hungry, and I'm determined,
And God shows me the way.

You Gotta Win

I'm starting on this journey, it's tough along the way.

There are no shortcuts or detours, no room to go astray.

Don't know where the road is going, but I know that it will end.

Preparation is the key, when you know You Gotta' Win.

The early morning wake-ups, they have their rightful place.

You have to start somewhere if you plan to finish the race.

You won't be distracted when the obstacles begin.

No room for doubt or excuses, when you know You Gotta' Win.

The commitment to study and train makes every day so long.

You must have the intestinal fortitude, and mentally be strong.

A burning desire and discipline, these traits will be your friend.

You better have a great supply, when you know You Gotta' Win.

There are many other tasks, which we do throughout the day.

To complete duties and chores, we have to find a way.

To finish is the aim, regardless of where you begin.

You'll be the last one standing, because You Gotta' Win.

With God at the forefront, your future is clear and bright.

Your focus is on the prize, your heart and mind are right.

You will not be defeated, you won't break or bend.

God gets the praise and glory, you know You Gotta' Win.

Humble Warrior

The Humble Warrior I am,
A present state of mind.
I'm built to make things happen,
No greater warrior you'll find.

Disappointments brought on humility,
I heal and get better as I climb.
I'm changing up the process,
The Humble Warrior state of mind.

Toughness is the base foundation,
To be nasty, an absolute must.
Relentless in my pursuit of greatness,
In God alone, I trust.

This journey will not be easy,
I don't expect it to be.
I have a sniper mentality,
So don't you mess with me.

I won't accept mediocrity,
Your weaknesses I will expose,
I'll break your will to win,
Challenged, so I rose.

I'm on a warrior's mission,
Can't lose and won't be denied.
The drive and will to finish,
And God, only, by my side.

The Humble Warrior on this mission,
No time for fun and for games.
You can't beat me, join me,
You won't ever forget my name.

No Guts, No Glory

No Guts, No Glory,
We have to take a stance.
We have to make this team,
The best in all the land.

No Guts, No Glory,
We will stand and fight.
We will get the job done,
And we will get it done right.

No Guts, No Glory,
We have the faith and drive.
The courage and hope to steer us,
For perfection, we must strive.

No Guts, No Glory,
There's no easy way to get there.
We are locked and loaded for battle,
We're ready to prepare.

No Guts, No Glory,
This is where it all begins.
We're ready to conquer the challenge,
We're fighting until the end!

Don't Forget About the Past

You are blessed with a good life,
It just happened so fast.
While you're enjoying this season,
Don't Forget About the Past.

Don't know from whence you come,
No, it wasn't quite a blast.
But I am here to tell you,
Only things in Christ will last.

You're shining so bright,
Remember what you've been through.
The past from which you came,
Paved the path just for you.

The moms and the dads,
From many years long ago.
Endured many hardships,
Giving you a chance to grow.

Enjoy the fruits of your labor,
Go and have a grand time.
But keep the things that you've gone through,
In the back of your mind.

And now that you've made it,
To the top of the stairs.
Someone helped you,
So help somebody else get there.

Just remember if you forget,
And get lost in your wealth.
Life is not worth living,
When you're alone by yourself.

So keep this chain going,
And the way to make it last.
Don't turn your back on your people,
And Don't Forget About the Past.

The Best Is Yet to Come

You've done it the right way,
You have your bling to show.
This is just the beginning,
You still have room to grow.

As you work and strive for greatness,
And think about what you've done,
Keep in mind just one thing,
The Best Is Yet To Come.

Self-motivation is your stronghold.
Let discipline be your guide.
Your desire will keep you focused.
To Dominate is your Drive.

You can accomplish all things,
With God as your friend.
No matter what the haters say,
He's with you until the end.

Know that they're always watching,
They know where you are from.
Commitment, Effort, Toughness,
The Best Is Yet To Come!!!

About The Author

Kerry Stevenson is the author of this spirit-filled motivational poetry book. You will find that Stevenson's poetry is full of encouragement, motivation, and thankfulness. In his influences, he hopes to help give counsel to friends and family in the areas of love and life. He is inspired to motivate and encourage all with his poetry. This is his first time he has used poetry on this scale to touch the lives of others. He is a lifetime educator who has always written poetry as a hobby. He is a Math teacher, where he has taught all subjects of Math on the secondary and post-secondary level. He received a Bachelor's Degree in Mathematics and a Master's Degree in Math Education from Alabama Agricultural and Mechanical University in Normal, Alabama. He received an Educational Leadership certificate in Educational Administration from Samford University in Homewood, Alabama. He and his wife, Tracy, have two children, Aisha and Jaylon. Stevenson was also a very successful high school football coach. He led his team to two state championship games in the state of Alabama in 10 years while coaching at Vigor High School. There were also three other years where his teams would make it to the state semifinals in the same sport.

Stevenson was officially selected to Nick Saban's staff at the University of Alabama in February 2013 to be the Director of Player Development. In the five years Stevenson has been in that role, the football team has won three SEC Championships and two National Championships — at the time of this book going to press.

Inspirations in Life

The publication of this book was made possible, in part, by the support of all of my family and friends. Thanks for your love, support, and encouragement. I would like to extend a special thanks to eVision, LLC (www.eVisionLLC.net) for your professional help, direction, and expertise in helping to make this dream a reality.

Kerry Showed Me How God Works

I never would have thought that going on a tour of the Alabama football complex would lead me to meeting one of the most inspirational people. Poetry always had captured my interest, and when Kerry said he made poems, I was all for it. I had no clue his poems would change the way I saw myself and the world. They spoke to me in a way that no one else had. I had doubted myself for so long, but his words told me that everything was gonna be okay. That the future holds so much and tough times are just obstacles to something great. I know that's true because people like Kerry are standing where they are today. He showed me how life is supposed to be lived. All through God and for him. Because God does everything for a purpose much bigger than us. I'm now stronger in trust that God is guiding me through life because Kerry showed me how. I'll never forget him and that day.

From Nikki Hammond

Inspirations in Life

Not many poetry books are written by football coaches, but this is one that was written over time with inspiration from Faith, Family, Friends and Football. Kerry's strong faith is clearly illustrated throughout all four categories.

Some poems were written definitely as a result of inspiration from key people in his life. It is especially interesting to me that some were written from Kerry to those he is mentoring. I think readers will especially enjoy those written during his tenure on the Alabama football coaching staff.

Bill Battle, former UA Athletics Director